Survival Communication:

15 Proven Tips to Stay in Touch With Your Family

Table of content

Introduction

Life is totally unpredictable. It is full of surprises for you – some good, some bad. But this is its ultimate beauty as well. After many happy moments, one disaster can come your way. You may become vulnerable and confused in handling such a situation. Therefore, it is vital to equip yourself ahead of the disasters and emergencies. Don't wait for them to arrive at your door.

First thing that you need to do is to prepare an emergency kit or a disaster bag for yourself. You can add in it things that you think will be highly helpful in the tough times such as match boxes, flashlights, whistles, dry food cans and much more. But there are very little details that you can miss out.

Similarly, it is important to prepare a survival plan beforehand. Decide a safe location to take shelter in, route to reach there and get regular supplies there. You must also plan for coming back to your home from there after the disaster. Don't forget to include your family and pets in the survival plan.

Also, you need to know to send signals either via electronic devices such as radios and walkie-talkies or through non-verbal communication methods such as lighting fire and blowing whistles. This book will provide you with all the required information.

Chapter 1. Arrange Emergency Radios To Stay In Touch

Hopefully, you would never need to rely on any kind of emergency radios in your life but if you are preparing an emergency kit then emergency radios are a must-have part. Not all of them are alike, and getting one reliable emergency radio is not that simple. Here are some points to keep in mind when buying one for you.

https://i.kinja-img.com/gawker-media/image/upload/s--MEJsxluM--/ c_scale,fl_progressive,q_80,w_800/lsn9bsftxfz6cz7b0mrp.jpg

Choosing a Reliable Emergency Radio:

Emergency radios are available in all kind of shapes and sizes. It is not a commodity that you can just grab from the shelf and put in your emergency kit.

There are some things that you need to consider before picking the one:

- What type of frequencies you need in your emergency radio?

- Does the one you are buying have a flashlight or light?

- Which power sources are supported by the emergency radio in your hand?

- What kind of batteries is included in this model? Regular or rechargeable batteries or none?

- Can other appliances such as your mobile phone or MP3 player be charged by this emergency radio?

- Does this model of emergency radio have a siren or glow light to let you find it in dark situations or other people find you?

- What is the size of the radio?

- How heavy is it?

- How sturdy is it?

- Is it packable or not? If yes, how much?

Select and buy an emergency radio for your disaster kit keeping these considerations in your mind. It will make the new purchase a helpful and skillful addition in your emergency kit. Let's have a detailed look at some of the features an emergency radio must possess;

Basic Emergency Radio:

Always buy an emergency radio with the feature of delivering alerts to National Oceanic and Atmospheric Administration and other signals to the outside world. NOAA is a scientific action group monitoring all kind of weather and providing your TV stations with satellite images that they use for their own programs.

A NOAA radio becomes your direct source of receiving progressive reports of the weather. Therefore never buy a two-way radio which may also be referred to as a shortwave radio. There are two main things you can do with an emergency radio in a disaster. First is, obviously, trying to communicate with others. The second purpose is to use an as a power-sipping connection to others. A basic emergency radio with NOAA alerts and other signals is perfect to achieve the first purpose while for the later one you need standalone AM/FM radio. NOAA alert is sent through AM radio. You can also use it to tune into the local FM radio stations to keep yourself updated. In the case of a severe disaster, you will need one with longer range to acquire complete information.

Radios Offering Specific Alert Messaging Decoding:

Specific Alert Messaging Decoding or SAME is the technology that allows to you to customize some specific locations for emergency alerts and other warnings. It will get you notified whenever there are certain disaster alerts and warnings for your specified location.

It is a digital code or protocol that used to send a 1050 Hz warning tone and encoded alerts for audible receptions on radios already equipped with receiving such kind of alerts and warnings. It can also send visual alerts and messages depending on its model and specific features. It is important not only for weather updates there can be other severe and potentially hazardous situations as well where an emergency radio with SAME technology can be handy.

Emergency Radios Supporting Multiple Power Sources:

A good emergency radio must have two ways to get powered up, at least. Better one must have more. Therefore always choose an emergency radio that supports not only multiple power sources but the advanced and modern ones are supported by it as well. Some of them are battery operated while others run on solar panels. Battery operated emergency radios are good as long as you store additional batteries in your disaster kit as well because batteries usually run dry on sitting in the device for too long. A hand cracking or other manual charging sources are good as well. Similarly an emergency radio supporting external power supply such as direct AC outlet plug in makes a good addition in your emergency kit. But better emergency radios are the ones that come in models supporting all of these power sources;

DC Batteries

Basic AC outlet

Charging Dynamo or hand cracking power

Solar charging panels

That is the ultimate power back up! Sometimes, other options such as USB ports and lights are also included to aid you in regular survival needs. Therefore, it is important to always buy an emergency radio that supports all or most of the power sources to get charged if you want to stay connected to your family when the world around you goes silent.

Life is completely unpredictable and this is its ultimate beauty. It is a good strategy to hope for the best but be ready for the worst. Preparing an emergency kit in advance is a good thing to do. Emergency radios are inevitable to be included in it. Now, you know the one you need to buy for your disaster kit.

Chapter 2. Walkie-Talkie Can Be Your Friend

A walkie-talkie is a handheld transceiver. It developed during the World War II. It was first used in infantry and then in tank units and field artillery. While after the war ended, these two-way radios were spread in the fields from public safety to jobsite work.

It is a half-duplex device for communication. That means that only one radio can transmit on a channel at one time but many can listen. It usually remains in receiving mode and thus receives any incoming messages and codes. However, to talk to it or to send your message, warning or alert to the others, just simply press the "push to talk" button on your transceiver. It will switch the device from receiving mode to the sending mode and thus enables you to spread your word.

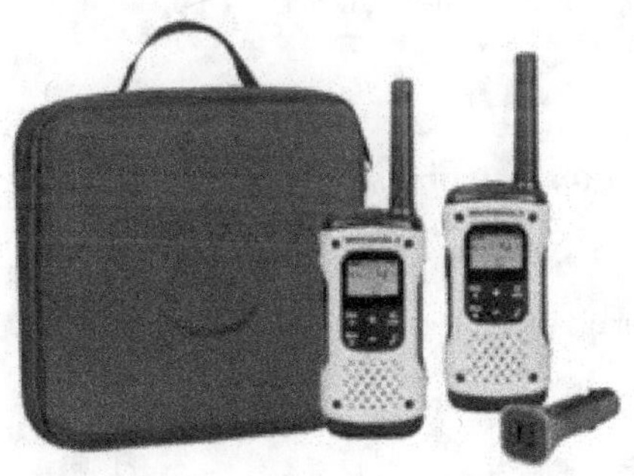

A typical walkie-talkie appears like a typical telephone handset. They are, however, slightly larger than them but they are a single unit. With an antenna mounted on its head, a walkie-talkie can send and receive signals to a far distance. Its earpiece is usually loud enough to let the user be heard. It has built-in speaker that can easily be heard by the user and all present in his immediate vicinity. It can be used to communicate with each other, or to a base station.

Walkie-talkie set is an inevitable addition in your disaster kit. It comes real handy when the power goes out and you are unable to find any kind of communication method. Walkie-talkie set becomes your new best friend in such a dark situation.

Buy a walkie-talkie set for your emergency kit is not an easy thing to do as it may appear at once to anyone. The reason is that it is a technical device and it requires a little bit of technical information to choose the ultimate set for you.

Six questions to answer before you buy one set for your disaster kit are:

- How far do you intend to transmit your message?

- How many channels do you desire?

- What kind of batteries will be needed in the new set?

- How handy your users can be?

- Are your devices compatible to pair together?

- How good is the warranty?

A large variety of different types of walkie-talkie set with wild features are available in your local market. Here we are discussing types of walkie-talkies in respect to their features;

Walkie-talkie **with Far Reaching Transmission.**

Not all details provided in the manuals of the walkie-talkie sets are right in their origin. Therefore, don't believe instantly on all of the information written in the sales literature when selecting a set for your disaster kit. The reason is that the distance calculated by the manufacturers is usually measured in an area with vacuum and sound travels faster and farther in vacuum. But in an area with buildings, trees, traffics and other interferences it is not possible for you to achieve the exact results. Two types of radios can help in this scenario. One is FRS i.e. Family Radio Service and the other is GMRS i.e. General Mobile Radio Service.

Walkie-talkie **with Multiple Radio Channels.**

Multiple radio channels are usually available in cities. Many are allotted to different areas already. Similarly, a business might have allotted different radio channels for different business functions. Whatever the case is, decide how many channels you want your radio to have especially when you intend to add in your preparedness for a disaster kit. It is crucial. Most of the walkie-talkies are either

FRS or GMRS that shows that use multiple channels, for instance, GMRC uses channels from number 15 to 22.

An important point to remember is that many walkie-talkie sets also offer privacy codes. These codes can block you outside chatter on a specific channel. Further remember that the calls are not private and anyone can listen to them. the only privacy you get is that your calls cannot be interrupted by anyone.

Walkie-talkies with Batteries.

Walkie-talkie run on batteries as this feature makes them portable. It is important to know the kind of batteries that the new addition in your disaster kit is going to need for power supply. These radios come with a large variety of power supply options. Some of them use AA or AAA regular alkaline batteries that are disposable while others might be using rechargeable batteries. Remember that in a disaster, there might be no electricity supply available for you to charge your Walkie-talkie sets and once, the rechargeable battery is out, you will be out as well. Therefore, buy walkie-talkie sets with disposable batteries and also stock such batteries in your emergency kit so you don't run out of power supply anytime during the disaster. Also don't install batteries in your set while it is just kept placed in your kit because batteries automatically drain on being kept in the device for too long.

Good warranty, compatibility of the set with other devices and the handiness of the users must also be kept in mind along with the number of supported channels, distance coverage and type of power supply sources while buying walkie-talkie radios for your emergency kit. Technology evolves everyday therefore also check for new available options too.

Chapter 3: Codes And Ciphers For Communication

Cryptography plays a major role in secret communication. It is the science of developing methods to conceal the real meaning of your message by using ciphers which is a method of hiding your message by replacing its letters with other letters or symbols. Different codes for secret communication are also developed under the same umbrella. Here's how you can create your own secret codes, ciphers and languages. Let's have a look!

Method # 1: Creating Standard Code:

Simply follow the following steps to create a standard code for you.

Step # 1: Create a Code Book:

Create your own language. Make words, patterns or phrases and replace them with the original alphabets. It is important to keep them sensible. Compile them all together into the form of a book. Your very own and private code book is ready! You can also share it with your family members and friends. Next step is to create a message.

Step # 2: Create a Message:

Once your secret code book is ready, create a secret message using the codes from the book. Create this message carefully. Follow all patterns, codes and phases from the code book. Remember that you can also pair your message with cipher. This will make it even more secured and safe. Once the message is carefully drawn, now is the time to translate it.

Step # 3: Translate the Message:

When you have created your message, deliver it to the concerned person. That person will now translate your secret message. For this purpose, he may need your code book. Give him a copy. It is important to tell him if you are using double encryption method in creating messages from your code book.

Similarly, you can translate a whole book in to codes. Just select a book and change the words with numbers. And then get it translated by your family members and friends. You can also develop police codes in this way. Simply pick a phrase or a sentence that you use more frequently and assign codes to them. Then memorize the codes. Now you can use them at anytime.

Method # 2: Developing Ciphers:

There a number of ciphers that you can develop. Here we will discuss one of them in step wise detail. Have a look:

Step # 1: Making Ciphers for Dates:

Simply pick a date, for instance 26-05-2016. Write down the date as: 05/26/16 i.e. with numbers and slashes. Take out the slashes now and write it down as: 260516. Now you have this six digit number that you can use to encipher your message.

Step # 2: Allot Numbers:

Now assign numbers to alphabets. Write the six digits over and over again until you reach the end.

Step # 3: Encipher Your Message:

Write down your secret message from left to right. And write down the numbers under it. Shift each letter to the next place as per the number under it. For example, if the number is 2 and alphabet is B then shift B to the place of D.

Step # 4: Get Your Message Translated:

Send your message to a family member or a friend and get it translated by them. They will need your ciphers. Provide them so they can decrypt and translate your secret message.

Similarly you can create number ciphers and Caesar shifts as well. They all work out so well and help you create your personal collection of secret languages.

Method # 3: Secret Languages:

You can create many secret languages such as Pig Latin, tap code and gibberish. They are all fun and help you creating a secret world of languages. Here we are discussing secret language Pig Latin.

Step # 1; Identify Words Beginning with Vowel:

If the word you intend to use starts with a vowel such as apple, then simply add ay in the end of the word like "applay".

Step # 2: Identify Words Beginning with Consonants:

Similarly identify words starting with consonants. If the word you intend to use start with a consonant then shift first two letters of the word to the end of it and add ay in the end. For example, glass will become "assglay" and bottle will become "ttleboay".

Step # 3: Speak Your New Secret Language:

So now you are ready to use your new secret language. It will be difficult to speak it in the beginning but with the passage of time, you will become its master. It sounds real good when you speak it fast. For that you need to practice so keep practicing.

Codes and ciphers help a lot in emergency situations. Since you have had been practicing it with your family members and friends over a long period of time, they all know, understand and remember most of the codes, ciphers and languages created by you. This helps them understand the secret message and thus reach you. Also codes and ciphers are smaller than regular message thus you are able to use less space in the sending message. This allows you to send more details than a regular text.

Chapter 4: Prepare a Survival Communication Plan In Advance

It is vital to make sure that your whole family is ready and conversant within the event of a disaster or emergency. You cannot always be along with them when these events happen therefore you should have plans to face such kind of disasters and emergencies. Also make sure that you're able to contact and find each other. Don't forget your pets in whole of the situation. They will be more worried than you. Here is how you can get mentally equipped for such an unfortunate event;

Prepare Yourself:

Before anyone else, prepare yourself to face any kind of disaster or emergency. Remember that you are going to survive the situation only if you are well planned and ready ahead of the event. There are certain steps that you can take in such a situation. Let's have a look;

Before a Disaster:

According to the American Red Cross, you must be taking the following steps in any of such events;

Have a meeting with your family and household members.

Discuss and decide the type of disasters and emergencies you are expecting to face in such a situation.

Get prepared accordingly.

Assign responsibilities among all the available members.

If any of the family members is in army then decide how you will carry out things if he or she gets deployed.

During the Disaster:

If you get separated:

You can get separated from your family members and friends and fellows during a disaster. This happens very commonly.

Here is what you should do if you get separated from the closed ones during a state of emergency:

- Decide two places to meet, for instance,

- Exactly outside your home in case of a fire.

- Outside your neighborhood if you are unable to return to your home or have been asked to evacuate.

- Select a person to contact who resides outside the area of disaster. You can text or call him from your mobile phone or through internet if the local phone lines have gotten out of service or are overloaded. It is important to keep emergency contact information saved in your phone or written in a diary.

- If you are asked to evacuate: You can also be asked to evacuate in the cases of emergencies and disasters. In that case, take the following steps;

- Select the place where you would go in such a situation.

Also decide the route through which you will reach at your safe haven. You can choose a motel or you can decide to stay with your friends or some family members living outside the area of the disaster. You can also opt for an evacuation shelter in case you don't find any other place to go instantly.

It may sound crazy but practice to evacuate. Yes! Practice to evacuate your home at least twice a year. After evacuation, drive to your destination through a specified route. Also mark other alternative routes on your map to reach the destination in case the original or the shortest one is impassable.

Also plan for your pets. Keep a list ready of the pet friendly hotels or rest houses or animal shelters or any living place which is ready to welcome your pets along with you on your evacuation route.

Inform your family and friends about your safe arrival at the destination.

Prepare Your Family and Pets:

It is not necessary that you are already with your family at the time of a disaster or an emergency. Therefore, always preplan about such events and get your family prepared as well. Plan ahead. There are certain steps that you must include in your plan to deal with any such event.

Step # 1: How to react at a safe place.

Step # 2: How to contact each other in such a situation.

Step # 3: How to get back to your home.

Step # 4: What to do in different kinds of situations.

Always plan and get prepared before a disaster or emergency arises. Don't wait for it to come first. Most important thing is to collect reliable information sources, alert and warning systems in advance. Remember that family communication, both before and during the disastrous situation is very important. Have meetings with them and consider everyone including your pets, if any. It is vital to know complete addresses and correct contact information of the workplaces and schools of your family members. It allows you to contact them with either physically or on call during a state of emergency.

You would have to evacuate on a minute's notice. Therefore, always keep your emergency kits and disaster bags ready. Also make complete list of places where you can go and take shelter in such situations. Also remember your pets. Don't plan to go to a place which is not animal friendly unless it is the last option for your survival.

Relief workers and volunteers will start reaching at the place of disaster only after it has occurred. Therefore, being prepared beforehand is inevitable important. You won't be having any time to find out the supplies, locate your pets and go for shopping. It is vital to have planned ahead. It will save your time and life both. Life is precious, protect it.

Chapter 5. Non-verbal Signals For Communication

Phone lines and GPS can die during a situation of disaster. You can get off the radar anytime during a state of emergency. But that does not mean that you cannot communicate with your loved ones. Thankfully man, over the time, has developed many non-verbal signals which you can choose to communicate with others during any kind of emergency or disaster. Here we are discussing some of them in detail. Let's have a look;

http://cdn.instructables.com/FDE/N0DA/IC7HNMVZ/
FDEN0DAIC7HNMVZ.MEDIUM.jpg

Non-verbal Signal for Communication # 1: Fire

If you don't have any type of electronic device to communicate with others then firing is the best and the most used non-verbal method to let other know about your location. Keep it well built and it will attract a lot of sights in every direction. It can also attract an airborne rescuer such as helicopter etc. as well.

Fire being used as a non-verbal communication signal is very much different from the regular fire such as cooking fire and camp fire. Therefore it is important to keep the differences in mind so that when you lit the fire as an emergency alert, it gets effective and attract as many sights as possible.

Step # 1: Evaluate your resources:

See around and collect as much dry wood as you can. Then start collecting items that you can burn. If you can find some sort of fuel then you can lit an effective fire in no time.

Step # 2: Place the gathered material:

Place all of the gathered material in large, open space on the ground in the shape of an elevated platform. For that, you can place three stronger woods in the shape of a bone fire arrangement.

Step # 3; Put on the fire:

Now pour the fuel, if you had found any. Find some tinder like an old bird's nest or dry grass. Lit it up and put it in the heap of woods. You need fire that burns slowly and emits a lot of smoke. Therefore, you can use wet leaves and alike things too.

Non-verbal Signal for Communication # 2: Visible Signals:

You can also build signal mounds to attract people towards the area of disaster. These mounds consist of three large rocks that are usually arranged in the shape of a triangle and place in an open area that is clearly visible from the sky. Rule of thumb is; the taller, the better. The reason is that taller mounds can be seen more easily from a longer and higher distance than the smaller ones.

Another choice is using flashlights. You can also use strobes. You can send signals by flashing light in SOS words if you have a specific target to send the signal to. You can use a reflective mirror or metal for signaling out your location as well.

After you get sure that your signals have been successfully sent, you must try to understand the signal being sent back to you completely. For example during night time, a flashing light can respond back or an airplane can fly over head and move back and forth during the day time.

Non-verbal Signal for Communication # 3: Audible Signals:

You can also opt for noise based signaling if you are unable to find material for fire or a flashlight to pass on your signal related to your location to others. The rule of thumb is here is the famous rule of threes. For example, if you possess a firearm and want to use it for audible signaling then shoot it three times consecutively. Remember to keep a space of 5 signals between each signal. This will help others to understand and it is a signal and not just a festive light. Another important point to remember is that it is an audible signal therefore people are going to hear it and then come to you following it. Therefore, let them hear one shot clearly before firing another one. This will let them follow the sound and reach you. Also don't maintain a longer space between the shots. This will make people think that you are trying to hunt any bird or animal and is firing after missing your first shot.

A whistle can help you out if you don't have a gun. Almost everyone has a whistle in his back. Therefore, it is more easily found than a firearm. Again, the rule of threes is to be followed. You need to whistle three times consecutively with a space of five seconds between each blow. People are going to listen to your whistle and follow the sound to reach you. Keep it steady and alarming. Its added advantage is that it takes less effort than other signals. Above all, it will never run out of ammunition. If you are lucid enough under any situation to take out the whistle and put it in your mind then you will be able to get people reach you by blowing it steadily.

Disasters and emergencies are uninvited guests. They never inform before arriving. Therefore it is very much important to be mentally and physically ready to face any kind of such situation. It may sound strange to you but it is good to keep practicing to lit fire without fuel and match box, similarly practice to blow whistle steadily. All these practices come real handy in any disastrous situation.

Conclusion

No matter if the world is ending any sooner or not, disasters and emergencies just keep coming back and forth. They are uninvited guests and do not usually pass out any kind of warning signs and alerts before coming. Therefore, it is vital for every sensible person to stay ready to face such situations.

Not only that you keep yourself ready but also prepare your family, close friends and pets as well. You can prepare an emergency kit. Make a complete list of the nearby places where you can take shelter in emergencies and which are also pet friendly so you can take your pets along. Also keep contact details of people whom you can rely on in disasters.

Life is a precious thing. Protecting it in every which way is our responsibility. Therefore, plan ahead instead of waiting for any disaster to reach you.

OR Go to this URL

http://zbit.ly/1WBb1Ek